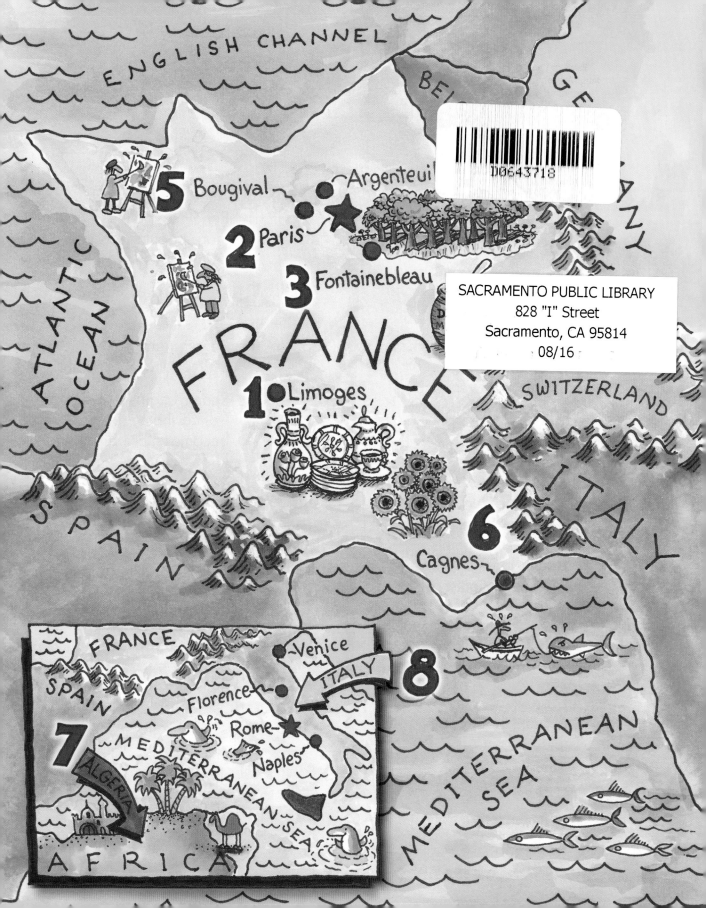

SACRAMENTO PUBLIC LIBRARY
828 "I" Street
Sacramento, CA 95814
08/16

D0543718

TIMELINE OF PIERRE AUGUSTE RENOIR'S LIFE

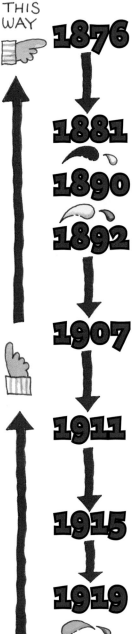

1841 Pierre Auguste Renoir is born in Limoges, France.

1845 The Renoir family moves to Paris. Pierre Auguste attends grade school.

1854 Renoir becomes an apprentice to a porcelain painter. He learns the art of painting flowers and portraits on vases and dinnerware.

1862 Renoir decides to study painting more seriously. He joins the studio of well-known artist Charles Gleyre. Renoir meets Claude Monet and other future Impressionist artists.

1865 Renoir leaves Gleyre's studio to paint outdoor scenes. He sometimes paints alongside Monet in the forests of Fontainebleau, and paints scenes along the Seine River in Argenteuil and Bougival.

1874 Renoir shows his work at the first Impressionist exhibition.

THIS WAY

UP HERE

1876 After years of hard work, Renoir's paintings become more popular. He starts selling many of his works.

1881 Renoir travels to Algeria and Italy.

1890 Renoir marries Aline Charigot, his model and assistant.

1892 Renoir begins to suffer from arthritis, and painting becomes more difficult for him.

1907 Renoir has a house and studio built in Cagnes. The warm weather there improves his health for a while.

1911 Renoir's health worsens and he has to work from a wheelchair. Still, he continues to paint some of his best works.

1915 Renoir has a studio built in his garden so he can work outside without traveling.

1919 Pierre Auguste Renoir dies at his home in Cagnes at the age of 78.

GETTING TO KNOW THE WORLD'S GREATEST ARTISTS

PIERRE AUGUSTE
RENOIR

WRITTEN AND ILLUSTRATED BY MIKE VENEZIA

CONSULTANT MEG MOSS

CHILDREN'S PRESS®

An Imprint of Scholastic Inc.

*For Rhea Sprecher. May your boating parties
continue to have many more lunchons.*

Cover: *Gabrielle and Jean.* 1895-96. Oil on canvas, 65 x 54 cm.
Collection Jean Walter and Paul Guillaume, Musee de l'Orangerie,
Photo by Hervé Lewandowski/RMN-Grand Palais/Art Resource, NY

Library of Congress Cataloging-in-Publication Data

Names: Venezia, Mike, author, illustrator.
Title: Pierre Auguste Renoir / Written and Illustrated by Mike Venezia.
Description: Revised Edition. | New York : Children's Press, 2016. | Series:
    Getting to know the world's greatest artists | Includes bibliographical
    references and index.
Identifiers: LCCN 2015037159| ISBN 9780531216682 (library binding : alk.
    paper) | ISBN 9780531221075 (pbk. : alk. paper)
Subjects: LCSH: Renoir, Auguste, 1841-1919–Juvenile literature. |
    Painters–France–Biography–Juvenile literature.
Classification: LCC ND553.R45 V46 2016 | DDC 759.4–dc23 LC record
available at http://lccn.loc.gov/2015037159

No part of this publication may be reproduced in whole or in part, or stored in a retrieval
system, or transmitted in any form or by any means, electronic, mechanical, photocopying,
recording, or otherwise, without written permission of the publisher. For information
regarding permission, write to Scholastic Inc., 557 Broadway, New York, NY 10012.

©2016 by Mike Venezia Inc.

All rights reserved. Published in 2016 by Children's Press, an imprint of Scholastic Inc.
Printed in the United States of America 113

SCHOLASTIC, CHILDREN'S PRESS, and associated logos are trademarks and/or
registered trademarks of Scholastic Inc.

1 2 3 4 5 6 7 8 9 10 R 25 24 23 22 21 20 19 18 17 16

Portrait of Pierre
Auguste Renoir
by Frederic Bazille.
1867. Oil on canvas,
24 2/5 x 20 inches.
Musee d'Orsay, Paris,
France. Photograph
by Erich Lessing/
Art Resource, NY.

Pierre Auguste Renoir was born in
Limoges, France, in 1841. He helped
invent Impressionism, one of the
most popular styles of painting in
the history of art. Even when he was
older and had painful arthritis,
Renoir loved to paint, and filled his
pictures with warmth and happiness.

The Impressionists enjoyed painting nature and joyful scenes of everyday life. Artists such as Claude Monet, Alfred Sisley, and Camille Pissarro weren't interested in details. They used quick brush strokes to give the feeling of a group of people, or a river, or a village, the moment they saw it. They also wanted to show how sunlight changes the color and look of things throughout the day.

The Parc Monceau, by Claude Monet. 1878. Oil on canvas, 28 5/8 x 21 3/8 in. The Metropolitan Museum of Art, Mr. and Mrs. Henry Ittleson, Jr., Fund, 1959. (59.142). Photograph by MalcolmVaron. © 1984/87 by The Metropolitan Museum of Art.

The Seine at Port-Marly, Piles of Sand, by Alfred Sisley. 1875. Oil on canvas, 21 $\frac{2}{5}$ x 29 in. The Art Institute of Chicago, Mr. and Mrs. Martin A. Ryerson Collection, 1933.1177. Photograph ©1994, The Art Institute of Chicago. All Rights Reserved.

The Red Roofs in the Village, Winter Effects, by Camille Pissarro. 1877. Oil on canvas, 20 $\frac{7}{8}$ x 25 $\frac{1}{4}$ in. Musee d'Orsay, Paris, France. Giraudon/Art Resource, NY.

In one of Renoir's most famous paintings, *Le Moulin de la Galette,* you can almost feel the sunlight flickering through the trees as the leaves move gently in the breeze. This was Renoir's *impression* of what he was seeing.

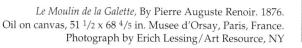

Le Moulin de la Galette, By Pierre Auguste Renoir. 1876.
Oil on canvas, 51 $1/2$ x 68 $4/5$ in. Musee d'Orsay, Paris, France.
Photograph by Erich Lessing/Art Resource, NY

When Pierre Auguste Renoir was
four years old, his family moved from
the small town of Limoges to Paris,
the capital of France. They rented an
apartment near the Louvre, the royal
palace of King Louis-Philippe and
Queen Marie-Amélie. Renoir saw the
queen quite often when he played his
favorite game of cops and robbers in

the courtyard of the palace. Part of the royal palace was a museum where people could see the great paintings and sculptures collected by the rulers of France. As a young man, Renoir spent many hours in the Louvre studying the works of the old masters–Europe's greatest artists from the 1600s and 1700s.

Even when he was very little, Pierre Auguste Renoir loved to draw. His father, a tailor, could hardly ever find the chalk he needed to mark directions on his fabric. This was because Pierre Auguste was always using the chalk to draw pictures all over the tailor shop, including the floor! Mr. and Mrs. Renoir never seemed to mind, and thought their son's artwork was pretty good.

When Pierre Auguste was 13
years old, his parents arranged
for him to get a job in a workshop
painting decorations on china
plates, cups, and vases.

At first, Pierre Auguste painted decorative flowers around the borders of the pieces. Later, he was promoted to painting portraits of famous people on the china. He learned about delicate colors and how to be a good craftsman.

Renoir was making pretty good money at the workshop, and later got other painting jobs that let him use his talent.

When he was about 20 years old, Renoir decided he would stop working so that he could study art more seriously.

He joined the studio of a well-known artist named Charles Gleyre.

Vase d'Arezzo, designed by Albert Ernest Carrier-Belleuse; painted by Henri-Lucien Lambert. Hard-paste porcelain, enamel decoration and gilding, with copper alloy mounts, 1884-85. Height: 33 2/5 in. The Art Institute of Chicago. Gift of the Antiquarian Society, 1991.313. Photograph ©1994, The Art Institute of Chicago. All Rights Reserved.

The Bath, by Charles Gleyre. 1868. Oil on canvas, 35 $1/2$ x 25 in. The Chrysler Museum of Art, Norfolk, Virginia. Gift of Walter P. Chrysler, Jr., 71.2069.

Gleyre taught his students to paint and draw as the old masters had done. This was the style of the day, and the most likely to be accepted by the *Salon*, the yearly official government art show.

The Death of Socrates, by Jacques Louis David. 1787. Oil on canvas,
51 x 77 ¼ in. The Metropolitan Museum of Art. Wolfe Fund, 1931. Catharine Lorillard
Wolfe Collection. ©1980/95 by The Metropolitan Museum of Art.

In France during the 1800s, it was important for an artist to have his work accepted by the Salon. Art collectors only liked to buy artwork that was approved by the Salon's judges. The types of paintings that were shown were usually carefully painted with dark colors and solid

Napoleon I in Royal Garb, by Jean August Dominique Ingres. 1806. Oil on canvas, 102 $3/10$ x 64 $1/10$ in. Musee de L'Armee, Paris, France. Giraudon/ Art Resource, NY.

outlines. Often, they showed a historical event or ancient legend, or were portraits of important people. Renoir enjoyed learning about these paintings in Gleyre's class, but some students felt the style was much too old-fashioned.

The Painter Jules Le Coeur in the Forest of Fontainebleau, by Pierre Auguste Renoir. 1866. Oil on canvas, 16 1/2 x 11 3/8 in. Museu de Arte, Sao Paolo, Brazil. Giraudon/ Art Resource, NY.

Three of Renoir's friends and classmates, Claude Monet, Alfred Sisley, and Frederic Bazille, wanted to try new ways of painting. Claude Monet invited his friends to join him in the nearby forest of Fontainebleau to paint pictures of nature outdoors.

Renoir decided to go because even though he enjoyed what he was learning in Charles Gleyre's studio, he also liked the exciting new idea of painting natural scenes outside of a dark studio. At the time, no one really painted outside. Some artists might sketch scenes outdoors for ideas, but they would always finish their paintings back in the studio.

Renoir and his friends would often discuss their new ideas at local cafés and restaurants. These meetings were important for the young artists. Renoir made this picture of his artist friends at the Inn of Mother Anthony. They may have been discussing how different colors look in the changing sunlight, or how putting their paint on thickly with quick brush strokes might add life to their work.

Some of the artists painted and sketched pictures on the walls of Mother Anthony's Inn just for fun. Renoir included one of his own sketches in the upper left corner.

Mother Anthony's Inn, by Pierre Auguste Renoir. 1866. Oil on canvas, 76 $^3/_{10}$ x 51 $^1/_2$ in. Nationalmuseum, SKM, Stockholm, Sweden.

La Grenouillere, by Claude Monet. 1869. Oil on canvas, 29 $^3/_8$ x 39 $^1/_4$ in.
The Metropolitan Museum of Art. Bequest of Mrs. H.O. Havemeyer, 1929. The H.O.
Havemeyer Collection (29.100.1112) ©1980/94 by The Metropolitan Museum of Art.

One day, Renoir and Monet decided to paint some scenes of an area near Paris where people went to have a good time boating and swimming. These are some of the earliest Impressionist paintings ever done. Renoir and Monet tried things they had discussed at their

La Grenouillere, By Pierre Auguste Renoir. c. 1869. Oil on canvas, 25 $^9/_{10}$ x 31 $^4/_5$ in. Nationalmuseum, SKM, Stockholm, Sweden.

café meetings. Working outdoors in the sunlight, both artists used bright colors and quick brush strokes to make their scenes seem sparkling and alive. The paintings look natural and unposed, and have a feeling of fun the moment it was happening.

Even though Renoir loved the look of his new works, he still did paintings in the older style just to get into the Salon show. Some of these works, like *Lise with Sunshade*, were accepted. But because the Salon would never accept the new Impressionist paintings, Renoir and his friends decided to put on their own exhibition. One of the paintings that Renoir showed at the first Impressionist exhibit is shown on the next page.

Lise with Sunshade, by Pierre Auguste Renoir.
1867. Oil on canvas, 72 $2/5$ x 45 $1/5$ in.
Folkwang Museum, Essen, Germany.
Photograph by Eric Lessing/Art Resource, NY.

La Loge, by Pierre Auguste Renoir. 1874. Oil on canvas, 31 1/5 x 5 1/4 in. Courtauld Institute Galleries, London Great Britain. Scala/ Art Resource, NY.

Pierre Auguste Renoir couldn't wait to find out what the public would think of his new paintings, but things didn't go very well. Most people didn't like the new works at all. They thought that the paintings were sloppily done, and that the artists didn't pay any attention to detail. Some people thought the artists were playing a joke on them, or that they might even be crazy!

Madame Georges Charpentier and her Children, Georgette and Paul, by Pierre Auguste Renoir. 1878. Oil on canvas, 60 $1/2$ x 74 $7/8$ in. The Metropolitan Museum of Art, Wolfe Fund, 1907. Catharine Lorillard Wolfe Collection. (07.122) ©1992 by The Metropolitan Museum of Art.

Fortunately, a few people in Paris did think the Impressionists' works were quite good. One wealthy businessman asked Renoir to do some portraits of his family. Soon, other people asked Renoir to paint portraits for them. Pierre Auguste

Renoir enjoyed doing these paintings, and was glad to be making money, but he also wanted to continue working on larger outdoor scenes of people having a good time.

A Girl with a Watering Can, by Pierre Auguste Renoir. 1876. Oil on canvas, 39 1/2 x 28 3/4 in. National Gallery of Art, Washington, D.C. Chester Dale Collection, ©1995 Board of Trustees.

The Luncheon of the Boating Party, by Pierre Auguste Renoir. 1881.
Oil on canvas, 51 x 68 in. The Phillips Collection, Washington, D.C.

Renoir often had his friends sit as
models in his larger outdoor paintings.
The lady holding the little dog in
Luncheon of the Boating Party soon
became Renoir's wife.

Pierre Auguste was happy to marry his favorite model, Aline Charigot. They had three sons, Pierre, Jean, and Claude.

Gabrielle and Jean, by Pierre Auguste Renoir. 1895. Oil on canvas, 25 1/2 x 21 1/4 in. Musee de l'Orangerie, Paris, France. Giraudon/Art Resource, NY.

Now Pierre Auguste Renoir could choose from a whole family of models!

Claude Renoir Playing, by Pierre Auguste Renoir. 1905. Oil on canvas, 18 1/8 x 22 in. Musee de l'Orangerie, Paris, France. Giraudon/Art Resource, NY.

Landscape on the Coast, near Menton, by Pierre
Auguste Renoir. 1883. Oil on canvas, 25 $^{7}/_{8}$ x 32 in.
Courtesy, Museum of Fine Arts, Boston, Massachusetts.
Bequest of John T. Spaulding.

Fruits from the Midi, by Pierre Auguste Renoir. 1881. Oil on
canvas, 39 $^{9}/_{10}$ x 25 $^{7}/_{10}$ in. The Art Institute of Chicago.
Mr. & Mrs. Martin A. Ryerson Collection. 1933.1176. Photograph
©1994, The Art Institute of Chicago. All Rights Reserved.

*Two Sisters (On the
Terrace),* by Pierre
Auguste Renoir
1881. Oil on canvas,
39 $^{2}/_{5}$ x 31 $^{4}/_{5}$ in.
The Art Institute of
Chicago, Mr. and
Mrs. Lewis Larned
Coburn Memorial
Collection. 1933.455.
Photograph ©1994,
The Art Institute
of Chicago.
All Rights Reserved.

Occasionally, Renoir would paint landscapes and still lifes, but his favorite subjects were always people. He loved to show the joy of life in his paintings.

Meanwhile, the public was finally starting to realize how beautiful the Impressionists' paintings were. But after years of hard work, and just when things were going great, Renoir decided to change his painting style!

Renoir felt he had done all he wanted to do with the Impressionist style. He wasn't exactly bored with it–he just thought it was time for something new. He decided to look for a way to use some of the things he had learned from studying the old masters years before. He tried combining their carefully drawn shapes with the light and bright colors of Impressionism.

In *Umbrellas*, you can see how Renoir started to change things right in the middle of a painting. The lady and two girls on the right are done in the Impressionist style, with quick, feathery brush strokes and delicate colors. The people on the left side, as well as the umbrellas, look smoother and seem more like solid objects. Renoir painted them using duller colors and solid outlines.

Umbrellas, by Pierre Auguste Renoir. 1886.
Oil on canvas, 70 $^7/_8$ x 45 $^1/_4$ in. Reproduced by
courtesy of the Trustees, The National Gallery, London.

Woman Tying her Shoe, by Pierre Auguste Renoir. c.1918 Oil on canvas, 19 4/5 x 2 1/5 in. Courtauld Institute Galleries, London, Great Britain. Samuel Courtauld Collection.

Renoir kept working to find just the right style of painting that would satisfy him. Near the end of his life, he finally seemed happy with his work. Just before he died, at the age of 78, he told a friend, "I think I'm beginning to understand something about painting."

The works of art in this book came from the following museums:
The Art Institute of Chicago, Chicago, Illinois
The Chrysler Museum of Art, Norfolk, Virginia
Courtauld Institute Galleries, London, Great Britain
Folkwang Museum, Essen, Germany
The Metropolitan Museum of Art, New York, New York
Musee de l'Armee, Paris, France
Musee de l'Orangerie, Paris, France
Musee d'Orsay, Paris, France
Museu de Arte, Sao Paulo, Brazil
Museum of Fine Arts, Boston, Massachusetts
National Gallery of Art, Washington, D.C.
National Gallery, London, Great Britain
Nationalmuseum, SKM, Stockholm, Sweden
The Phillips Collection, Washington, D.C.

ANSWERS

1. **TRUE** As a teen, Renoir had a job painting detailed decorations and portraits on vases, dishes, and teapots. He was encouraged to work quickly and got used to painting at a super-fast pace. Renoir created more paintings than any other Impressionist artist.

2. **b** Jean Renoir was a filmmaker. His movie *The Grand Illusion* is considered by many film historians to be one of the greatest movies ever made.

3. **TRUE** Because of painful arthritis, Renoir was unable to model or shape clay. Renoir created sculptures by directing a young sculptor to mold clay figures according to his instructions.

4. **a** Young Pierre Auguste loved to sing. His parents provided him with private lessons, and he was even offered a position in the chorus of a Paris opera company. But even though his music teachers thought he could have been a professional singer, Renoir chose art as his life's passion.

5. **c** When Renoir and Monet scraped together enough money for food, they usually bought a sack of dried beans. The cooked beans were filling, and a sack of them would last about a month.

6. **TRUE** Pierre August Renoir tried to live as simply as possible. For most of his life, he had just a few pieces of furniture and a skimpy wardrobe. He threw out anything that was old or worn out. Renoir felt the same way about his artwork, and often got rid of drawings and watercolors he didn't think were worth keeping around any longer!

LEARN MORE BY TAKING THE RENOIR QUIZ!

(ANSWERS ON THE NEXT PAGE.)

1. TRUE OR FALSE:
Pierre Auguste Renoir made over 5,000 paintings during his life.

2. Pierre Auguste wasn't the only famous Renoir. His son, Jean, was also world-famous. What was Jean Renoir known for?
a He manufactured the first line of affordable French automobiles.
b He was a filmmaker.
c He was the only son of an Impressionist artist to swim the English Channel.

3. TRUE OR FALSE:
Renoir created sculptures without ever touching one.

4. Aside from painting, what was another one of Renoir's talents?
a Singing
b Horse whispering
c Miming

5. A young Pierre Auguste Renoir and Claude Monet shared a small studio apartment space for a while. They had very little money and could afford only one basic food. What was it?
a Frozen yogurt
b Moon pies
c Dried beans
d Fried okra

6. TRUE OR FALSE:
Renoir sometimes used his drawings and watercolors to light his wood-burning stove and fireplace.